# Poems from the Heart

## A Collection of Poems

# Richard F. Gery

*Illustrated by Barbara Williams, Gary J. Gery, Charla Morse, and Richard F. Gery*

**VANTAGE PRESS**
New York • Los Angeles

Published by Vantage Press, Inc.
516 West 34th Street, New York, New York 10001

Manufactured in the United States of America
ISBN: 0-533-09022-9

Library of Congress Catalog Card No.: 90-90062

To my loving wife, Darlene,
who instilled the confidence in me to write this book

# CONTENTS

# Preface

The poems in this book were all inspired by various events that the poet has experienced.

You will note that on some pages beneath the poem is an explanation as to what inspired the poet to write that particular poem. The poet believes by doing this the reader may better understand the feelings of the poet when the poem was written.

# My Dearest

My dearest, between us there are many miles,
   in which there are valleys and streams.
I would give anything for one of your smiles,
   like the kind I see in my dreams.

My dearest, although for a while we will be parted
   and will suffer heartaches like this,
Our happy life had already started
   on the night of our first kiss.

My dearest, the times when I'm not there
   and you are feeling sad;
Remember, in mind and heart we are always near;
   then things won't seem so bad.

My dearest, there are many lonely nights,
   but our hearts will stay aglow,
With the hope of a wonderful future
   and a love that will always grow.

*The poem "My Dearest" was written in 1954 when the poet was in the U.S. Army. It was revised slightly to its present form in 1989.*

# Hold My Hand, Lord

Hold my hand, Lord, and show me the way.
Keep me from falling, help me through the day.

Hold my hand, Lord, my heart and eyes open wide,
to your beautiful world, with you at my side.

Hold my hand, Lord, and be my perpetual light.
Lead me through darkness, keep me in your sight.

# Friends

Friends are people who are always there.
By their actions, friends show that they care.

Friends ask for nothing, except a smile or a glance.
They ask few questions and leave nothing to chance.

Friends live by the golden rule as we all should do.
They give of themselves with a love that is true.

Friends are with you during good times and times of pain.
Their friendship is given freely, without thought of
personal gain.

Friends can come from all walks of life.
They are your neighbors, relatives, a husband or a wife.

# My Wife

All that I am and all that I've done
  throughout my adult life
Has been blessed with the courage
  and understanding of my wonderful wife.

  I have made mistakes, I have been depressed
    and have had moments of strife,
  Yet through it all, the good and the bad,
    my strength was there—in the form of my wife.

What can I say to express how thankful
  I am for my wonderful life?
My love for you will be for eternity,
  my precious, beautiful wife.

*This poem was written in June 1987, prior to the death of the poet's first wife, as an anniversary gift.*

*She was dying from cancer, and her illness inspired the poet to produce this poem.*

*A certificate of Honorable Mention was received when this poem was entered into a poetry contest.*

# A House

It took carpenters, bricklayers, and other tradesmen
   to mold such an imposing sight,
Roofers, plumbers, electricians, an architect,
   working together with all their might.

A combination of skills produced a house
   which stands on soil of sandy loam,
But, with care and pride a gentle little lady
   turned the structure into a loving home.

You made me feel like a king in a castle
   and my chair was my throne,
But since you're gone, it's just a house
   and I am so very much alone.

*After the poet's first wife died, he sold the large house they owned to buy something smaller and easier to maintain. His feelings regarding his house were brought out in this poem.*

# Little Angel

God said, Come home, little angel,
    I'll open my door;
Come back to me, precious child,
    and suffer no more.

Your loved ones grieve, my little angel,
    but they need not fear,
Because you will be together again
    in my loving care.

*This short, touching poem was written in January 1988 for a cousin of the poet who lost her eight-year-old son to leukemia.*

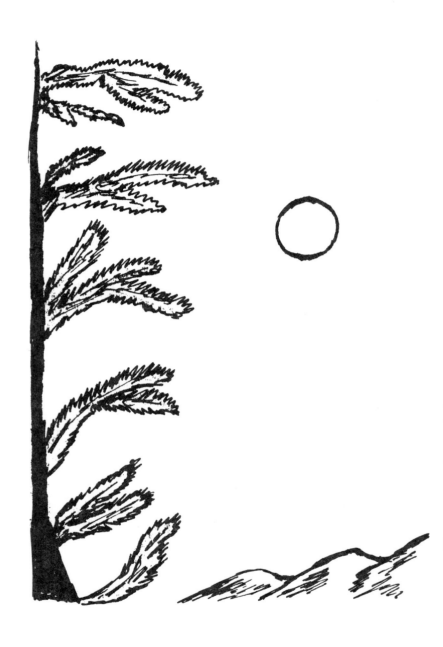

# Was It Hot Last Summer?

Was it hot last summer? I cannot remember.
My life was a blur from May to November.
Was it hot last summer? I would not know.
My life was in turmoil, we could have had snow.

Was it hot last summer? Did my grass turn brown?
I felt so empty, my world was crumbling down.
Was it hot last summer? Were the birds in song?
Everything that seemed so right suddenly was so wrong.

*It was Memorial Weekend in 1988 when the words for the above poem were contrived.*

*The poet recalled a year prior, when his first wife's illness was diagnosed. He then realized he had been living in a vacuum since her illness and death.*

# Grandpa Sam

In the northernmost region of Italy he was born.
It was a century ago on a beautiful morn;
While a young man he took Filomena as his wife.
They set sail for America and a bountiful life.

He traveled from the north shore of the Mediterranean
    Sea
To make his mark in the land of opportunity;
Lumber mills were in his blood for many years
He enjoyed happiness and laughter and shed a few tears.

He is a lover of life and its simple pleasures
The Giants, 49ers and a pipe are among his treasures;
Man can build a bridge, a skyscraper or a dam
But only God in his infinite love can create Grandpa Sam.

*The poem "Grandpa Sam" was written for an acquaintance in June
1988. The subject of the poem was celebrating his hundredth birthday,
and the poet was asked to write a poem in honor of the occasion.*

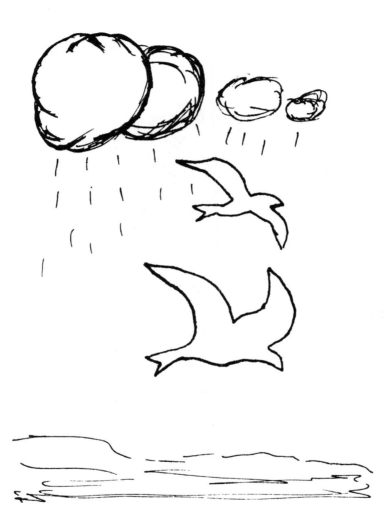

# Man's Best Friend

A dog is mischief and love
    all rolled into one;
He is happiness and laughter
    and hours of fun.

When you're feeling blue and
    your spirit is down,
He will pick you up and
    remove your frown.

You may scold him, ignore him,
    and send him away,
But just call his name and
    he's ready to play.

He senses illness, or when something
    is not right;
He will pour out his heart
    so you're not uptight.

A dog is loyal and with you
    to the end;
It's been said before, he is truly
    Man's Best Friend.

*"Man's Best Friend" was written one lonely evening when the poet was sitting home with his dog, "Sparky." The happiness he received from the dog's companionship inspired the words.*

# What You Mean to Me

It's hard to write what you mean to me.
  Just to be with you, makes my heart jump with glee.
The only one who knows how great our love
  is God, looking over us from heaven above.

I'll try, always, to tell you how much I care,
  for our love is one thing that will never wear.
My dear, another thing to you I must confess:
  I pray that we will have eternal happiness.

# Festival

Once again the time is here,
Time for fellowship—time to share.

People gather, young and old,
As the festivities begin to unfold.

Music, laughter, food and games,
And a plethora of ethnic names.

Colorful booths and many lights,
Wonderful smells, beautiful sights.

Let the fun begin, have a ball;
Come to the festival, one and all.

# My Precious Mother

I may have taken some things for granted through the
    years;
    I've tried to make you proud and not cause any tears.

You were always at my side whenever I needed you;
    I felt your caring and concern whenever I was blue.

We may not always agree on one thing or another;
    but I thank God for you every day, my precious mother.

*The poet sent the above poem to his mother for Mother's
Day in 1989.*

# Dad, Please Tell Me

There were many times through the years when I felt
    alone and sad
    because I felt worthless and unwanted and yearned for
    your love, Dad.

Through all the hurt and the pain and the tears,
    I tried to be special and hide all my fears.

There were good times too, which I will hold very dear,
    especially the fun of going to a ballgame to cheer.

I remember also—and I'm sure you've never been told
    you deserve credit because you have a heart of gold.

I'm not here to pass judgment because I do love you,
    but please, Dad, please tell me that you love me too.

*The above poem was sent to the poet's father on Father's Day, 1989.
The feelings of being unwanted as a child were a result of growing up
in an alcoholic family.*

# The Lady and Her Mechanic

It was before the Second World War
    when they met;
To say their love would be everlasting
    was a sure bet.

They were not born of royalty, and their
    possessions were few;
But their commitment to each other
    was genuine and true.

They worked together hand in hand
    and side by side,
And though they may have stumbled,
    they never broke stride.

This wonderful lady and her mechanic were
    molded by God's own hand;
No finer couple could be found here
    or in any other land.

*The poet has a favorite aunt and uncle who were always
there for him throughout his life. His uncle retired in 1987
after years of owning a service station. His aunt also retired,
for she handled all of the bookwork for their business. They
are a special couple.*

# Dear Aunt

She is soft as a rose petal and gentle as
    a summer breeze.
Her life is unassuming and simple,
    based on a desire to please.

She is loving and kind, with a touch
    of sentimentality too.
Her heart is warm and tender and to
    God she is true.

She lives by His Golden Rule and is not
presumptuous or bold.
When God created you, dear Aunt,
I'm sure He broke the mold.

*Written for the poet's favorite aunt and his wife's great-aunt,
both of whom have been a source of love and kindness to
them all of their life.*

# Wait for Me

Wait for me, please, give me time.
Everything seems so confusing yet so sublime.

The trauma of life unfolds each day.
I need answers as I kneel to pray.

Life goes on, it's been said to me,
A day at a time into eternity;

Wait for me, please, allow me some slack.
You're my answer and reason for coming back.

*Starting with "Wait For Me," the balance of the poems in this book were written for the poet's present wife, Darlene. This poem was the first one written for her.*

# It Feels So Right

When we're together and I hold you tight,
  I'm telling you, darling, it feels so right.

We talk and laugh and have such fun.
  We enjoy a moonlit night or noonday sun.

I want to be with you every day.
  My life is miserable when you are away.

The simple things in life mean so much:
  a kind gesture, a smile, your gentle touch.

I'll hold you forever with all my might.
  Don't fight the emotion when it feels so right.

# The Crossroad

We traveled our own paths for many a year,
   yet somehow, some way, our hearts felt so near.

Our journeys took us to the crossroad and
   immediately upon sight,
We knew deep down in our souls
   everything would be all right.

At the crossroad we discovered a new path in life,
   which we will walk together, forever, as husband and
     wife.

# Forgive Me

Forgive me when I falter or when I fail to smile.
You know me well enough to know that is not my style.

Sometimes life is quite complex and I try to right all
    wrongs.
However, the answers are not as easy as they are in many
    songs.

Amidst all the fuss and confusion, one thing I know for
    sure:
The love I have for you is eternal, endless, and pure.

Forgive me when I'm depressed, for it's not often that I'm
    down,
But knowing that you love me makes me smile, not frown.

*An "off" day prompted this poem, and the poet wanted his lady love to
know that it had nothing to do with her and he still loved her.*

# I Feel Like I Know You

I feel like I know you, sir—
though we have never met,
For you have been highly regarded—
on that you can bet.

Your daughter has compared me to you—
what an honor for me.
I hope I have your approval to
keep her through eternity.

Trust me with your daughter's future—
she'll be in my loving care.
Laughter, love, honesty, and tenderness
all will be ours to share.

I feel like I know you, sir—
so you need not fear.
As long as I am around, she
will not shed a tear.

*The poet wrote the above poem to his wife's deceased father, whom she
loved very much. She often compares the poet's attributes to that of her
father.*

# I've Loved You All My Life

Don't ask me why or how because it is difficult to explain.
To say I've loved you all my life might even sound insane.

I've known you forever, my heart and my soul seemed to
    say.
Since we first met, I yearned to be with you every day.

We both enjoy little things in life, things we hold so dear.
I've loved you all my life, and I'll always want you near.

# You Are

You are the sweet smell of a flower,
   and you grow more precious by the hour.
You are the warmth of a noonday sun,
   and you are life, happiness, and fun.

You are the beauty of a star-filled night,
   and you have the aura of a brilliant moonlight.
You are the magic of a total eclipse,
   which illuminates your tender, sweet lips.

You are refreshing, like a soft summer rain,
   and you are a rainbow touching my window pane.
You are as gentle as a butterfly at play,
   and you are mine forever, not just for today.

# Our Love Is . . .

Our love is overwhelming to be sure,
But it is special and will endure.

Our love is not pretentious or untrue.
It's honest and pure as morning dew.

Our love is based on tenderness and caring.
It is concern for each other, and sharing.

Our love is spontaneous and filled with emotion.
It's an abundance of laughter, humor, and devotion;

Our love is straightforward, natural, and sincere.
It is communication and understanding without fear.

Our love is simple, yet tasteful as wine.
It is most special because you are mine.

*The poet and his wife were engaged in November 1988, and the above poem was presented to her for Christmas 1988. This poem also received an Honorable Mention in competition.*

# I Look into Your Eyes

I look into your eyes and you intoxicate me;
I see your smile and it consumes me.

I feel the closeness of your body and I'm delirious;
I smell the sweetness of you and know this is serious.

I look into your eyes and you melt into my soul;
I drink in your beauty and love is taking its toll.

The nearness of you has my senses reeling;
I look into your eyes and get a wonderful feeling.

*The poet and his wife married in April 1989. After a beautiful evening at a dinner-dance, while driving home, they were expressing their love to each other. . . .*

# My Dream Is Simple

How I wish I could make all your dreams come true—
A trip to the stars, a voyage on the ocean blue.

I wish I could afford furs, jewels, cars or a yacht;
I'd give to you my sweet, beautiful lady, all that I've got.

My dream is simple—I want you to be at my side;
I want you there always as I show you off with pride.

All I can offer you is me, my love, and my life;
I'll protect you, care for you and love you forever, my
    sweet wife.

# This Is Our Life

Quiet evenings, lazy days, a home-cooked meal—
  this is our life, this is for real.

Our favorite restaurant or a getaway weekend—
  this is our life, the message we send.

Wine, soft music and a warm, tender embrace—
  this is our life, which no one can erase.

Shopping together, planning together, or enjoying an
    evening ride—
  this is our life, working side by side.

A well-planned vacation or one contrived in haste—
  this is our life, a love we both taste.

# My Heart and Soul

I'll always love you with my heart and soul,
And making you happy will be my continuous goal.

I am yours forever and you will always be mine.
Now that we have each other, our future will be fine.

I'll care for you and respect you in good times or bad.
We will always work together to make our life happy, not
    sad.

You are the beauty of a flower and the freshness of spring.
You are my ray of sunshine and you make my heart sing.

My dreams were fulfilled when God gave me you,
For He has given me a love that is so true.

I have really been blessed to have you enter my life.
I love you with my heart and soul, my darling, adorable
    wife.

*The poet read this poem to his wife after reciting his marriage vows.*

# From the Day We First Met

From the day we first met, I knew we were meant for
each other.
I felt the mingling of our lives as we made adjustments
for one another.

From the day we first met, I knew this was a very
special feeling.
The sensation I felt in my mind and body sent my
senses reeling.

From the day we first met, I couldn't believe my
intuition was true.
I felt like I knew you forever, for I was deeply in
love with you.

From the day we first met, and for the rest of my
humble life,
I will care for you, respect you, and love you, my
darling wonderful wife.

*The above was the second poem the author wrote to his wife, and it
received an award in a poetry contest.*

44

# Because I Have You

Because you're you, life is worthwhile.
You make it seem bearable because of your style.

The touch of your lips, the smile on your face,
The warmth of you near me in a loving embrace.

When life appears darkest, you make it feel fine,
And nothing else matters, as long as you're mine.

When everything seems dim, you bring out the light;
Then good things happen, and it seems so right.

I love you so much that it's hard to explain.
You quench the drought in my life like a gentle rain.

If ever I feel depressed, or lonely, or blue,
My spirit is lifted when I look at beautiful you.

It seems like I've waited an eternity or two.
My prayers were finally answered because I have you.

# I Am Blessed

I am blessed to have you enter into my life,
  for I was lost and life was not worth living.
Like a vision, or a dream, you were suddenly there,
  elegant, gracious, so full of life and so giving.

I am blessed to have found true love
  because that thought never entered my mind.
I am so very proud of you, my wonderful lady.
  Your beauty and charm make you one of a kind.

I am so blessed to have you for my own.
  You radiate goodness and kindness and all that is love.
Your smile shines on my soul and enriches me.
  Surely, you are sent to me by God above.

# The Union

There is no greater union than that of the union
  between husband and wife.
The melding of two hearts, two minds and two bodies
  into one;
The union of two people in love, in a very deep love—
  that is non-ending;
Sharing thoughts, sharing ideas, sharing dreams,
  walking through life hand in hand;
Being there for one another during good times and
  the not-so-good times;
To communicate, to be honest and up-front, and to treat
  each other lovingly;
To always want to be near each other, touching each other
  and enjoying each other;
A union built on these precepts will be forever.

# We Are Love

We are one heartbeat
We are one breath
We are one body
We are one life
We are all this, for we are love.

We are caring
We are sharing
We are kind
We are spiritual
We are blessed, by God above

We are tenderness
We are considerate
We are unique
We are togetherness
We are gentle, like a dove

We are one soul
We are one mind
We are one feeling
We are one thought
We are all this, for we are love

# Senses of Love

When I touch you, my whole being shudders in delight.
The feel of your beautiful, soft body lingers into the night.

The sweet smell of your femininity permeates the air.
I'm in ecstasy from the fragrance of your hair.

The very sight of you, your beauty and grace,
Makes my heart leap as I look at your face.

To taste your warm, soft lips sends my senses reeling.
Never before have I encountered such a wonderful feeling.

As I hear words of love and dreams we both share,
I know ours is a special intimacy that is so rare.

These senses of love, which we will always have,
Constitute the ultimate romance, which is yours and
        mine alone.

# Nothing Else Matters

The whole world stops spinning as our
    hearts beat as one.
Nothing else matters, for our love is
    second to none.

Knowing that I've loved you forever and
    you've always loved me,
Makes our love so special that it
    will carry on through eternity.

While others may lust for fortune, fame,
    material goods and power,
I want you and a love that grows stronger
    by the hour.

I believe we have the very best because
    I believe in you.
Nothing else matters, but us, our life,
    and a love so true.

# The Fairest of the Fair

You came along without warning;
  I wasn't looking and there you were.
With a surge of extra energy,
  my heart and body began to stir.

All sense of reasoning eluded me;
  I walked about in a state of confusion.
I can't believe what has happened.
  My life was touched by a wonderful intrusion.

When we affirmed our mutual love,
  I felt like I was walking on air.
How could I be so fortunate
  to have you, the fairest of the fair.

# Touch Me

Touch me, hold me, let me know you're mine.
Just the thought of loving you makes my life divine.

Touch my lips with yours, put your hands on my face.
The very nearness of you makes my poor mind race.

Touch me, put your arms around me, warm my heart.
I want you at my side always, never to be apart.

Your touch excites my body, my soul, and my mind;
And I know that our love is one of a kind.

# Concerts in the Park

Everyone enjoys concerts in the park, especially with
a gentle, summer breeze;
Blankets, pillows, and chairs strewn about amidst the
variety of beautiful trees.

People gather from all walks of life,
　　to enjoy an evening away from the strife.

Sandwiches, fruit, candy, and other delicacies brought
　　from home;
　　the popping of bottles and the enjoyment of
　　champagne's foam.

The sound of music fills the night's air,
　　bringing back memories, laughter, and maybe a tear.

Concerts in the park, peaceful and fun for young and old;
　　a chance to get away and relax and let your life unfold.

*The poet and his wife enjoy the summer concerts in the park. They
attend as many of them as possible.*